BAUSTEINE MAGIC

Activity book

4

Erarbeitet von
Christiane Doms,
Barbara Hardt,
Gisela Mazumdar-Rolando,
Ilka Paetz,
Carmen Probst
und Julia Quaedvlieg

Diesterweg

Contents

speak

write

read

look it up

draw

CD

listen and draw / write

listen and point

partner work

group work

game

craft work

song

Children around the world

1 Write the names of the children.

2 Where do they live?

3 Write about some children.

4 Play a riddle with a partner.

True or false?

	true	false
In December it is very hot outside.	SC	TH
In music classes I play the fiddle.	KL	HO

	true	false
I send my homework by email to my teacher.	Y	O
My favourite subject is Haddithi.	L	U

	true	false
At school I learn Kiswahili.	RD	AR
I never play cricket at breaktime.	IC	OU

	true	false
We don't use computers at school.	HA	ND
I never send emails to my teacher.	BE	TH

	true	false
I don't like music classes. They are terrible.	O	E
The fiddle is my favourite instrument.	WO	WH

	true	false
In the afternoon I go home by bus.	EA	RL
At breaktime I play cricket with my friends.	L	D

Answer: ____

1 Circle the correct answers.

2 Write and read the sentence.

School in Germany and school in Tanzania

What's the same?

We all go ______________________

______ learn ______________________

______ have fun ______________________

What's different?

We have got ______________________

____

We haven't got ______________________

____

They have got ______________________

____

They haven't got ______________________

____

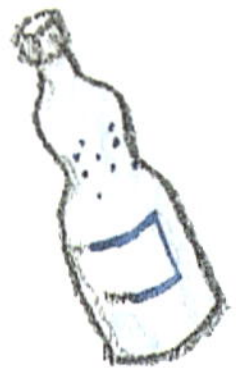  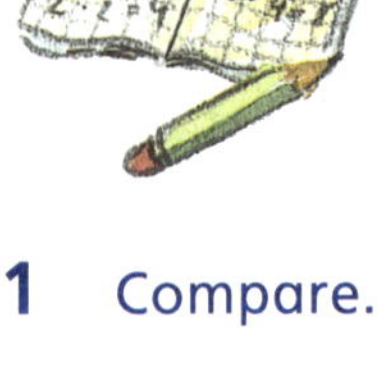  

German English
Maths PE RE
Music school uniforms
computers rulers
rubbers pens lunchboxes
pencils sharpeners
coloured pencils
glue scissors
drums pencil cases
at breaktime in class

1 Compare. What's different? What's the same?

2 Write about it.

Be a reporter

What's
your favourite subject?

Who's
your favourite teacher?

Who are
your best friends?

What do you like
to do at breaktime?

____
____

How do you
go to school?

1 Read the questions.

2 Write your own question.

My reporter sheet

Reporter: ______________________________

____
____
____
____
____

I interviewed: ______________________________

1 Write your own questions.

2 Do the interview. Write sentences.

Keep fit

We keep fit at school

movements → directions

movements → parts of the body

movements

______ ______
______ ______
______ ______
______ ______
______ ______

directions

______ ______
______ ______
______ ______
______ ______
______ ______

parts of the body

______ ______
______ ______
______ ______
______ ______
______ ______

1 Sort the words.

2 Can you add more?

walk	up high	dance	head	to the board	back
skip	jump	bend	to the door	legs	
feet	run	on the spot	arms	stretch	

Time for action

______
______
______
______
______
______

3 Find exercises. Write them down.

Merlin keeps fit

Merlin jumps. WE
Merlin walks. AR
Merlin sits. LS

Merlin sleeps. IF
Merlin runs. TH
Merlin bends his knees. KE

Merlin walks to the window. LO
Merlin walks to the door. EP
Merlin walks to the table. NE

Merlin touches his nose. FI
Merlin touches his knees. GI
Merlin touches his head. BY

Merlin jumps up high. P
Merlin sits on a chair. R
Merlin turns around. T

Merlin stretches his arms. AT
Merlin stretches his legs. IN
Merlin stretches his back. OU

Merlin plays soccer. CA
Merlin plays the keep fit game. SC
Merlin plays hide-and-seek. BE

Merlin throws a ball. LU
Merlin kicks a ball. TR
Merlin catches a ball. HO

Merlin runs on the spot. OS
Merlin hops to the door. IT
Merlin dances wildly. OL

Answer: ______________________________

1 Read the sentences and circle the correct letters.
2 Fill in the letters.

Be smart – protect yourself

For ice skating I need

______________________________.

For climbing I need

______________________________.

For playing hockey I need

______________________________.

For skateboarding I need

______________________________.

____

____

____

For playing football I need

______________________________.

For cycling I need

______________________________.

For in-line skating I need

______________________________.

____

____

____

1 What do you need to protect yourself? Talk to a partner.

2 Sort out and complete the sentences.

Are you fit?

name: ______________________________

age: ______________ height: ______________

When do you go to bed during the week? ______________

How often do you eat	every day	once a week	once a month	never
chocolate?				
fruit?				
ice cream?				
pizza?				
cucumber?				
tomatoes?				
crisps?				
hambuger?				

How often do you drink	every day	once a week	once a month	never
lemonade?				
water?				
tea?				
juice?				

How often do you	every day	once a week	once a month	never
do sports?				
play outside?				
play computer games?				

Type blue
You're really fit. Great. Keep just going like that.

Type yellow
Not bad. You're fit but you can do much better. Go for gold.

Type green
You like sport and healthy food. But perhaps you can do some more?

Type pink
You can do better. Exercise twice a week and drink more water and you'll be fit.

1 Do the questionaire. Which type are you?

2 Do an interview with your partner.

Planets

______________ is bigger than ______________

____

____

____

Saturn	an alien	a spacecraft	Venus
Earth	Mercury	the solar system	Mars

1 Write sentences.

Planets

It is yellow and brown.
It has got icy rings.
It is bigger than Mars.
It has got 62 moons.

It is planet ____________________

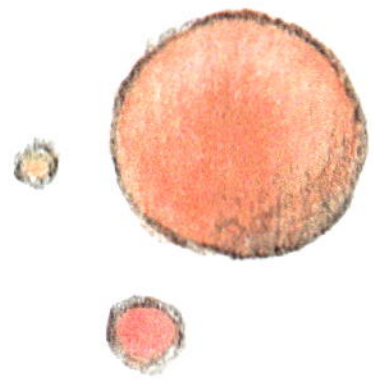

It is red.
It is very cold.

It is ____________________
It is smaller than
____

It is planet ____________________

It is ____________________
____
It has got ____________________
____
____

It is planet ____________________

____
____
____
____
____
____

1 Read and find out.

2 Write about two other planets and draw them.

3 Talk to your partner and let him guess.

Our Earth song

On our Earth there are flowers and trees.

On our Earth there are meadows and bees.

There are green fields and mountains so high

and the sea, the air and the big blue sky.

1 Read the song and draw pictures.

2 Sing the song.

3 Make up your own verse and draw pictures.

My planet

This is planet ______________________________

The colour of my planet is ______________________________

On my planet there are ______________________________

____

____

____

____

____

1 Draw your own planet.

2 How is life on your planet?

Pirates

Long ago, Blackbeard sailed from England	☐ to France. ☐ to the coast of Jamaica. ☐ to India.
His name was Blackbeard because he had	☐ two pistols. ☐ a red beard. ☐ a black beard.
Captain Blackbeard was	☐ a famous German pirate. ☐ an American sailor. ☐ a dangerous English pirate.
The name of his ship was	☐ "Queen Elizabeth". ☐ "Queen Anne". ☐ "Queen Anne's Revenge".
Pirates ate	☐ cheese sandwiches. ☐ bread and salted fish. ☐ fish and chips.
Blackbeard and his crew stole	☐ food and drink from the market. ☐ gold and silver from other ships. ☐ seagulls.
Blackbeard and his crew captured	☐ wild animals. ☐ many ships. ☐ parrots and turtles.
The crew worked all day because they had to	☐ sail, to clean and to cook. ☐ prepare a barbecue party. ☐ collect seashells on the beach.

1 True or false? Read the sentencees and tick the correct ending.

2 Compare with a partner.

All about pirates

Pirates sailed to ______

Pirates had got ______

Pirate's names were ______

Pirates ate ______

Pirates liked ______

Pirates stole ______

Pirates drank ______

Pirates captured ______

Pirates worked a lot. They ______

______

1 Complete the sentences.

2 Play "Pirates on deck".

Famous pirates

One-eyed Jack

He was a pirate of the Caribbean Sea.

Long John Silver

Anne Bonny

She had red hair.

Captain Blackbeard

Captain Hook

Calico Jack

was	dangerous a pirate (on the Caribbean Sea) big and tall famous

had	two pistols red hair an eye patch a hook for a hand a black beard a parrot

1 Write sentences about the pirates.

Wanted

He is ______________________________

____

small famous
big dangerous

He wears ______________________________

____

a shirt an eye patch
blue trousers an earring

He has got ______________________________

He has got ______________________________

____

brown hair black hair
an eye patch a red beard
green eyes only one eye
only one leg only one arm
pistols a parrot
a peg for a leg a knife
a hook for a hand

He likes ______________________________

____

turtles gold diamonds
salted fish silver

He ______________________________

____

1 Draw a pirate.
2 Give him a name.
3 Describe your pirate.

Shopping

1 What can you buy in the shops? Draw and label.

Special offers

1 Match the slogan to the picture.

2 Make your own slogan and draw a picture.

A shopping dialogue

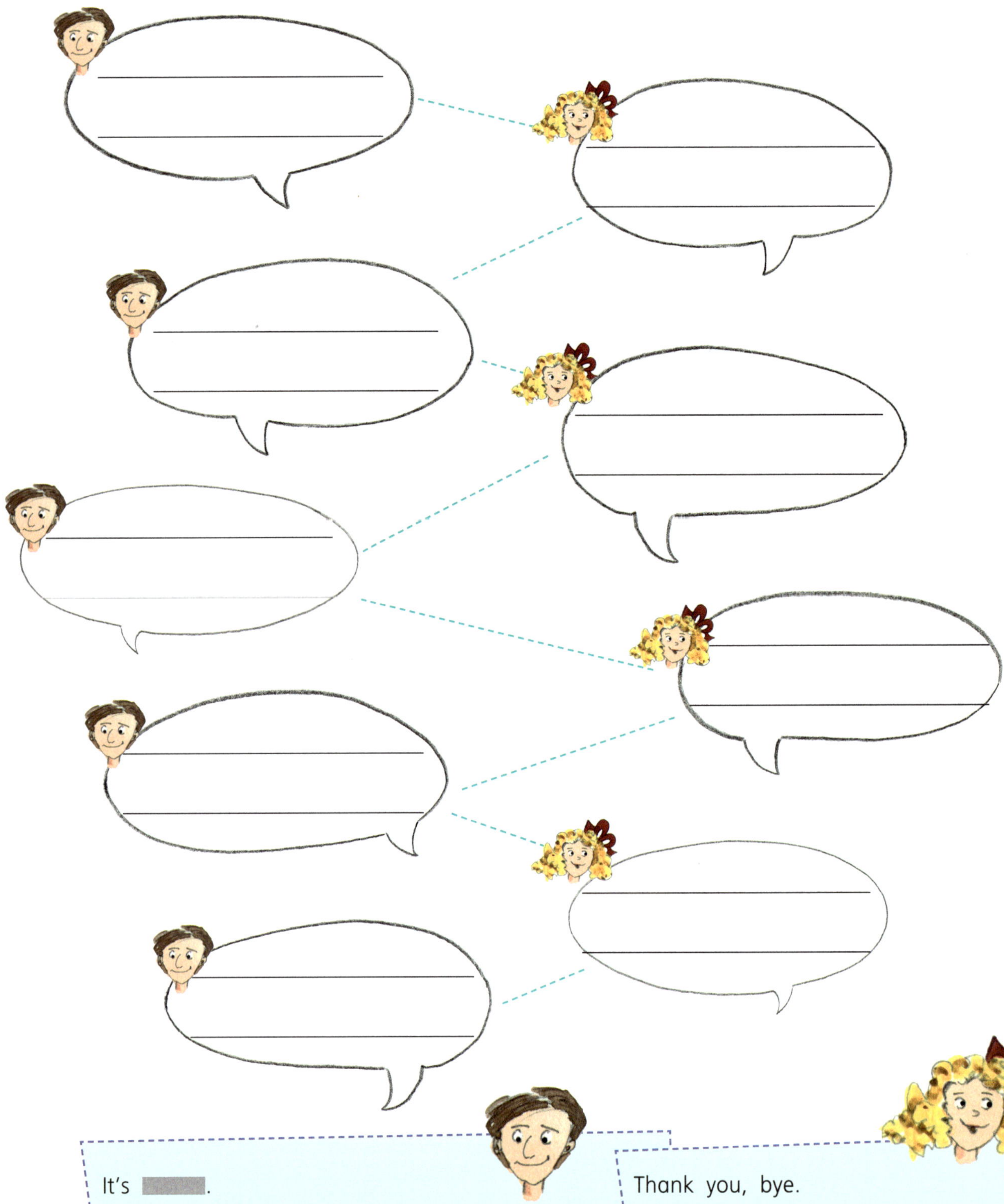

It's ____.

You're welcome. Have a nice day.

Hello. Can I help you?

How about this one?/How about these ones?/

This is cheaper. / These are cheaper. / They are on sale.

Thank you, bye.

That's too expensive.

I'll take ____ .

I'd like ____. How much is it?

1 Write a shopping dialogue. Choose sentences.

2 Read it with a partner.

The Magic Shop

Betty, Jack, Said, Sally and Tom go shopping.

They go to the Magic Shop.

Tom has got £6.00. Said pays £7.00.

Jack does not buy the ghost costume.

Said and Tom like reading books.

A girl buys the Halloween stickers.

Sally and Jack pay £10.00.

Betty	Jack	Said	Sally	Tom
ghost costume	Halloween stickers	juggling balls	book	magic hat

1 What do the children buy? Read and draw lines.

2 Compare with a partner.

King Arthur

A famous dragon

This is the famous dragon ______________________________

He has got ____________________ and ____________________

____

He is ______________________________________

____

He can ______________________________________

____

eyes	nose	claws	swim	mouth	tongue	
head	long	big	dangerous	run	fast	
sharp	body	strong	fly	teeth	tail	legs

1 Draw and write.

2 Tell a partner.

The famous King Arthur

King Arthur had a sword, a sword,
and Excalibur was its name.
He lived a long, long, time ago,
but we know him all the same.

King Arthur had a shield, a shield,
and Pridwwen was its name.
He lived a long, long, time ago,
but we know him all the same.

This is

King Arthur had a horse, a horse,
and Llamrei was its name.
He lived a long, long, time ago,
but we know him all the same.

King Arthur had a castle, a castle,
and Camelot was its name.
He lived a long, long, time ago,
but we know him all the same.

King Arthur had a knight, a knight,
and Lancelot was his name.
He lived a long, long, time ago,
but we know him all the same.

King Arthur had a Queen, a Queen,
and Guinevere was her name.
He lived a long, long, time ago,
but we know him all the same.

1 Listen to the ballad.
2 Write sentences.

At the castle

1 
2 
3 

1 ______________________________

2 ______________________________

3 ______________________________

4 
5 
6 

4 ______________________________

5 ______________________________

6 ______________________________

		to dress	
	learns	to play the lute.	in the yard.
Jane	cleans	the horses	in the stables.
Brian	feeds	to read and write	with Father Henry.
	plays	to fight	in the armoury.
	helps	the weapons	the queen.

1 What does Jane do? What does Brian do?

2 Write sentences.

My busy day at the castle

1 Describe your own day at the castle. Who are you?

2 Tell your partner about your day.

A message for you

Let's meet at 6pm. CU Katie

Lots of love 4U. Happy birthday.

UR so beautiful. Happy Valentine.

The new film was great. LOL

Sorry, I'm at work. TTYL

CU l8er :-)

I love U2.

1 Write the correct messages.

2 Write your own text message.

3 Let your partner guess.

U	you	R	are
2	too	l8er	later
4	for	TTYL	talk to you later
BRB	be right back	C	see
:-)	smiley	LOL	lots of laughs

Interview

How often do you ...					
name:	every day	once a week	once a month	only on holiday	never
send an email?					
send a letter?					
send a postcard?					
call someone?					
text someone?					

1 How about you? Fill in.

How often do you ...					
name:	every day	once a week	once a month	only on holiday	never
send an email?					
send a letter?					
send a postcard?					
call someone?					
text someone?					

How often do you ...					
name:	every day	once a week	once a month	only on holiday	never
send an email?					
send a letter?					
send a postcard?					
call someone?					
text someone?					

2 Do two interviews.

Sign in for a pen pal

My name	
My birthday	
My image	
My email	
I live in	
Message	

I live in ...
I've got ...
His/her name is ...
I like/I play ...
I like ... best/My favourite ...

family
friends
pets
hobbies
school

1 Sign in for a pen pal.

2 Present your profile in class.

Tom leaves a message

1 Complete the speech bubbles. Who does Tom call?

Hi Eliot, ____________________

____

____

____

____

1 Tom calls Eliot and leaves a message.

2 Act out a dialogue on the phone with your partner. This time you are both on the phone.

Jobs at the zoo

I'm the	cook. vet. secretary. shop assistant. caretaker. zookeeper.	I work	with animals. in the zoo shop. in the zoo restaurant. with animals. in the office. in the zoo.

1 Name the animals.

2 What do the people say?

They all work at the zoo

Tony

the ______________________

He feeds the

lo animals.

ga children.

so grandmothers.

Sheila

the ______________________

She eats rd

She buys uv

She sells rr souvenirs in the shop.

Gary

the ______________________

He waters the

n elephants.

y plants.

t visitors.

Costa

the ______________________

He sleeps ha

He eats er

He cooks dr in the zoo restaurant.

Calvin

the ______________________

He fixes

iv broken things.

co broken bones.

di broken hearts.

Valerie

the ______________________

She

ok feeds the elephants.

er looks after sick animals.

rd is the zoo director.

Who is missing? Leo, the ______________________ is missing.

1 Read the sentences and circle the correct answer.

2 Write the jobs. Who is missing?

A crazy day at the zoo

1 Work with you flip book. Write a text about a crazy day at the zoo.

My day with Tony the zookeeper

We meet Valerie at quarter past eight.

We tell her which ______________ are sick .

At ______________

we have lunch with Gary and Calvin.

1 Spend a day with Tony the zookeeper.

3 Read it to your partner.

Animals in danger

The wombat lives in Australia.
It lives in the forest.
It eats grass and plants.

1 Write about the animals.

1 Find more. Draw and write about them.

Why are some animals in danger?

People hunt the elephant for its tusks.

That's why the ______________ is in danger.

People hunt the ______________ for its ______________.

That's why the ______________ is in danger.

People hunt the ______________ for its ______________.

That's why the ______________ is in danger.

1 People hunt animals. Complete the sentences.

is getting smaller and smaller is getting warmer and warmer is getting more and more polluted	elephant eagle blue whale jaguar wombat panda bear polar bear turtle	fur feathers tusks	forest sea savanna polar desert mountains river jungle

Animals in danger

The jungle is getting smaller and smaller.
That's why the jaguar is in danger.

The ______________ is getting smaller and smaller.

That's why the ______________ is in danger.

____

____

____

____

2 Animals are in danger. Why? Write sentences.

Bears, bears, bears

The panda bear

- lives in forests in China in Asia
- is one and a half metres (1,5) tall
- has got black and white fur
- gets one or two cubs
- eats only bamboo

can climb trees

The polar bear

- lives in the Arctic
- is two and a half metres (2,5) tall
- has got white fur
- gets one to five cubs
- eats meat
- can smell very well

The koala bear

- lives in forests in Australia
- is half a metre (0,5) tall
- has got grey fur
- gets one cub
- eats eucalyptus leaves
- can hear very well

1 Choose one of the bears. Write about it.

2 Tell a partner about your bear.

All about black bears

1 Do you remember the speech bubbles? Write what you have to do.

Helping friends

I help ____________________ to ______________________________________

____

____

____

____________________ helps me to ____________________________________

____

____

____

feed the pet   repair the bike   work with the computer
clean   do the homework   lay the table
do the shopping   make breakfast

1 When do you help someone?

2 Who helps you?

All about Andrew

My name is Andrew and I am eleven years old.
In my family there are mum, dad, me and my sister.
Her name is Anne and she is seven.
I have got a big dog. His name is Benny.
We live in a small house in Newcastle.

I like sports a lot. On Mondays and on Saturdays
I play cricket in a team. I am good at running.
But I also like to go cycling with friends.
My favourite film is "Finding Nemo".
I like to go to the cinema.

The name of my school is St. George's Primary school.
My favourite subject is Literacy. I am good at writing stories.

We have got school dinners. My favourite food there
is pizza, but I don't like hot soup. I always burn myself.

That's Andrew

name: ____________________

age: ____________________

school: ____________________

pets: ____________________

favourite subject: ____________________

favourite food: ____________________

favourite sport: ____________________

hobbies: ____________________

1 Read the text and find out all about Andrew.
2 Write about Andrew.

A trip to London

S

O

B

1. The Queen lives here.
Guards protect the Queen.

Y

2. You can have a great view over London.
It is next to the River Thames.

3. It is next to Tower Bridge.
It is famous for the Crown Jewels.

R

4. Hop on and off
and see all of London.

O

5. It's the name of the bell.
The bell is bigger than a double-decker bus.

N

6. You can see famous stars
and take a photo with them.

____

____

____

L

N

D

Answer:

____

1 Read and match.

2 Write your own sentence.

Where's the thief?

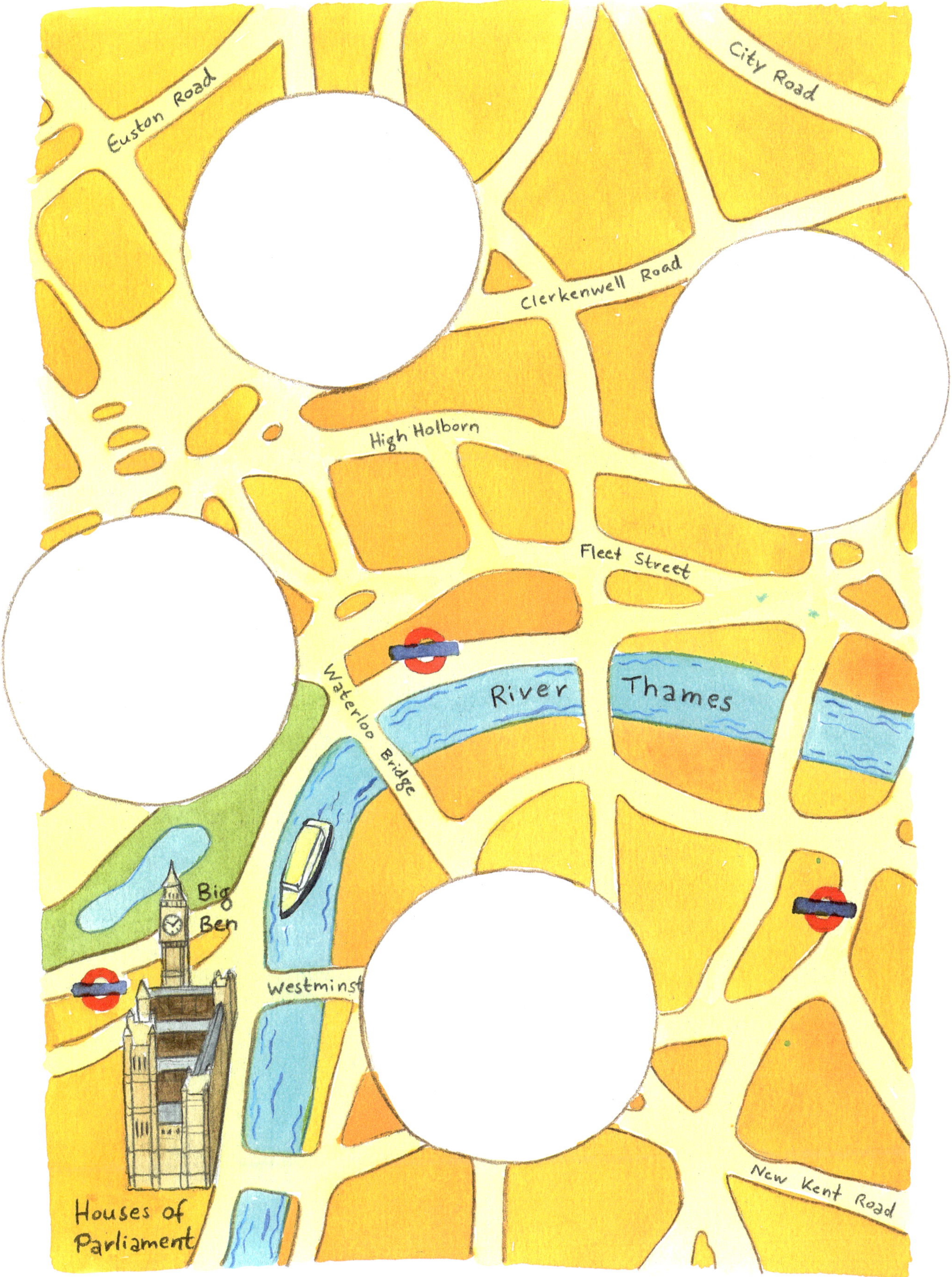

1 Where's the thief? Play with your partner.

Christmas in Australia

true	false	
SA	CH	Christmas in Australia is hot.
NTA	OR	Santa sometimes comes by surfboard.
IS	HE	The children get presents on Christmas Day in the morning.
A	O	The Christmas tree is never made of plastic.
N	S	Christmas is in summer.
R	T	The children make a snowman on the beach.
AR	HE	The children don't sing Christmas carols.
BE	IS	On Christmas Day people often have a picnic or barbecue on the beach.
A	O	The Jacaranda tree is in bloom in December.
TH	CH	Koalas sit in Christmas trees.

Answer: ____________________________________

1 Circle the correct answer.

2 Write the answer.

Write a poem

Christmas
very hot
Santa and surfboard
sitting on the beach
Australia

hot cold foggy frosty windy sunny stormy rainy ...
Santa surfboard angel presents candle Christmas tree snowman ...
sitting on the beach swimming in the sea singing on the rooftop riding on the sleigh ...

1 Read the poem.
2 Write a Christmas poem and read it to your partner.

Birthday

1 Fill in the months.

2 Ask your friends: "When is your birthday?" Fill in the names.

Months and seasons

Tom
birthday: 27.5.

1. Tom's birthday is on the ____________________

   That's in ____________________

   On his birthday he likes to ____________________

Peggy
birthday: 13.7.

2. Peggy's ____________________

   ____

   On her ____________________ she likes to ____________________

3. My ____________________

   ____

   On my ____________________ I like to ____________________

4 Find out and write.

5 Write about yourself.

> go swimming play football climb fly a kite
> have a costume party play basketball play outside
> have a barbecue play stop dance go to the cinema

Birthday planner

name			
In which month is your birthday?			
In which season is your birthday party?			
Who is coming to your birthday?			
What do you wish for your birthday?			
What do you like to do on your birthday?			
What do you like to eat on your birthday?			
What do you like to drink on your birthday?			

1 Ask your friends. Take notes.

2 Compare the results in class.

BAUSTEINE MAGIC

Activity book 4

Erarbeitet von
Christiane Doms, Barbara Hardt,
Gisela Mazumdar-Rolando, Ilka Paetz,
Carmen Probst und Julia Quaedvlieg

Illustriert von
Yvonne Hoppe-Engbring, Alexandra Junge
und Anke Rauschenbach

Druck A[1] Jahr 2010
Alle Drucke der Serie A sind im Unterricht parallel verwendbar.

Redaktion: Christine Pfeiffer
Herstellung: Nicole Hotopp
Umschlaggestaltung: Visuelle Lebensfreude, Hannover, Peter Pfeiffer (Illustration),
www.biolib.de (botanische Zeichnung), www.photocase.de (Hintergrund)
Typografie und Layout: Anke Rauschenbach, Annette Henko
Satz und technische Umsetzung: Druck- und Medienhaus Sigert GmbH, Braunschweig
Druck und Bindung: westermann druck GmbH, Braunschweig

ISBN 978-3-425-**02196**-6
ISBN 978-3-425-**02197**-3